quiet armor

quiet armor

POEMS

STEVIE EDWARDS

Curbstone Books / Northwestern University Press
Evanston, Illinois

Curbstone Books
Northwestern University Press
www.nupress.northwestern.edu

Printed in the United States of America

10 9 8 7 6 5 4 3 2 1

Library of Congress Cataloging-in-Publication Data

Names: Edwards, Stevie, author.
Title: Quiet armor : poems / Stevie Edwards.
Description: Evanston, Illinois : Curbstone Books/Northwestern University Press,
    2023.
Identifiers: LCCN 2023019284 | ISBN 9780810146464 (paperback) |
    ISBN 9780810146471 (ebook)
Subjects: LCSH: Women—Social conditions—Poetry. | LCGFT: Poetry.
Classification: LCC PS3605.D89856 E39 2023 | DDC 811.6—dc23/
    eng/20230425
LC record available at https://lccn.loc.gov/2023019284

For Daisy, Tinkerbell & Peaches

*I thought how unpleasant it is to be locked out; and
I thought how it is worse perhaps to be locked in.*
—Virginia Woolf, *A Room of One's Own*

I am out with lanterns, looking for myself.
—Emily Dickinson, *Letters of Emily Dickinson*

CONTENTS

≈

PARTHENOGENESIS

When my mother was young, she feared
she was such a good Christian girl

God might grow his new son inside her
like we plop seeds into the garden

without asking the soil its thoughts
on plumping up pumpkins & peas

& who would believe her? Sister
of the town's worst poison-headed

hooligans, she tried to do enough
good to make up for their transgressions—

joined a church that forbade dancing,
finished her homework, said her prayers

as if a family's fate balanced on a seesaw
& she could keep her brothers from

flinging off through the stratosphere
& never returning back to her on earth

from ether's heights. In New England
Aquarium an anaconda has borne fruit

of only her making. No contact with males—
her body wanted a child & made one.

Wonder of wonders, a child with only her
DNA slithers into the world. I haven't

conjured any miracles out of myself yet
in this lifetime. I fear I never will

be a witch or martyr. That I won't be good
or bad enough to warrant progeny

or remembrance. I used to want to turn
my pain into wine stains & watercolors

but now I want it not to touch
anyone, to keep it from brushing

my true love's arm. What if all I want
is quiet, a dog at my feet, television

remote in hand, half a turkey sandwich
with light mayo & orange cheese—

who will sing for me? Often I hope
nobody will. I'd like a good long sleep.

WINDOW SHOPPING

~

Maybe I could get married
if it meant that neckline—if it meant a deep plunge
just a freckle shy of the navel
                                        could be more goddess
than *Jersey Shore*, only then
could I say yes, drape
                          your lightest chiffon
down past my toes—yes, I will drag this ivory cloud
behind me like a glorious wheelbarrow
                                                for everyone
even my mother, to see
                          I've woven flowers in my hair.

~

But I am as uncertain of the designer
                as I am of white dresses. My mother wore one
down the aisle at twenty-one
                          & I never stop hearing about it:
the smallest size on the bridal shop's sale rack.
She did the alterations herself, took in her own waist.
                          I am always the teenage girl being told
Mom's dress is too slender for me.
                                There's always a measuring
tape wrapped around my waist.
                          I am holding my breath:
                this is the story of a tailor's daughter.
                                        Mom's wedding dress
chucked in the Goodwill box for *someone*
                          who can use it.

~

Once, my love stared at the pink numbered ribbon
            as I wrapped it gently
                        around our pit bull's neck
to check her collar size & he exclaimed *Oh, that's how
you measure bodies!* He'd never seen
                        a fabric measuring tape, only
                        the hardware store's stiff yellow.
Perhaps he imagined holding a string to a yardstick
                        to learn a human's true girth. Perhaps
he'd never considered it. The pup relaxed into my arms.
            I kissed her forehead, said
                        Who's a good girl?

~

I'd like to consider not knowing seam allowances—
            the shame of growing
                        beyond a dress's farthest edges.
I'd like to consider
                        not knowing size charts, how many
            inches in a size 8 waist, a size 4, a nothing size.
There were the years I could model
                        neon mountains
            of bedazzled prom dresses
                        while my mother examined
hems she'd sewn for other people's daughters.
There were the years I was too full
            to be useful.
                        Perhaps I could unknow them
like maps of cities I don't live in anymore.
            I could order a pain au chocolat at the coffee shop
                        stir real cream & sugar into my dark roast

& smile the whole time.
        Perhaps in Texas I've found
                the right distance: six state lines
away from my youth, I could love a chiffon gown
      in the window enough
                 to take a picture. I could gasp
    like the first time I ran fingertips down
a bolt of velvet & thought
              how queenly.

EASY AS PIE

My mother taught me to feel the dough in my hands & sense
its readiness with my fingertips, to know when to say *yes, this will do.*

The dough in my hands must sense I am a fruitless woman:
Don't you know when to say yes? Just follow the steps in order,

you futureless woman. It's a simple task. I've been raised
to follow her steps in order, first the ring & then the stroller.

It's a simple task. I've been raised to peel thin skins of peaches
off in small rings, to roll out the delicate Crisco dough

& peel back parchment paper like a Band-Aid off a small girl.
But my crude Crisco dough is too weak for the juice of peaches

like a soaked Band-Aid on a small girl. With readiness, her fingertips
covered in the juice of peaches, my mother taught me to feel.

LADYLIKE

~

In the backyard with my brother gathering
            brush to burn
in a smoky pile with December's desiccated
                  pine, Dad says I have to
put a shirt on, though the summer air is syrup
            thick & my brother roams
bare chested & I am six or seven & helping
            tidy the wild
& we have a wood-lined lot & long gravel drive
            & there is nobody
to see it, but I am a girl in this heat
                  & always will be.

~

At a football game wearing khakis I am alarmed
                              by the blood-riddle. I stuff my underwear
                with toilet paper, tie a sweatshirt around my waist & shiver
                         in the autumn dusk. I tell nobody
        my body's been visited by this
                              unwelcome guest. At home I scrounge
                 my closet for the single maxi-pad dispensed in health class,
smuggle stained clothes out with the kitchen trash.
                  Mom is certain it's drugs: What am I doing
                              with the bag, the trash, the night? Nothing.
          I am doing nothing, I say again & again.
                                She fishes out the evidence: the bloody
nothing my body has released into the night.
                                   & then she sits me down to tell me
           she didn't get her period until nearly fifteen
                      & mine has barged in early at eleven
                           because I am fat—
        my blue jeans & bras already grander than hers.
She hands me a pack of pads & tells me they are expensive
                                & I'll never stop needing them,
           to be careful of staining my school clothes.
                                  I tell her I'm sorry
              because I never know what else to say
                         for being fat, for not being a boy, for bleeding.

~

The first summer of my adult life
      without a thigh gap

& I've moved to the South to learn how raw
      flimsy skin scarcely touched

by sun can rub itself. *Like hamburger*,
      I want to sob to someone

over the phone. To a mother, but not mine—
      a fleshier woman

who can understand this new betrayal.
      Blood smears down

my legs walking home two miles
      in a gluey August heat

in a pencil skirt. Not my period, not
      an almost baby refusing

to voice its cries into hospital air, no new
      era opening, just too much

softness. Oh, how I wish to be done
      with the body,

Lord. Or I wish to be a serpent not
      an Eve, certainly not

another Adam. Please, let me slip off
      my old skin when it suits me

      & slither my own way.

NOBODY IS LOST

Nobody is alone. Nobody is stalking
the playground like it will disappear again

into the dust of teenagers & flame.
Nobody is tying the ribbons precisely

in her slippery hair. Nobody is missing
half her tiny teeth in the photo. Nobody

is eight. Nobody is baking fish sticks
& mac & cheese for family dinner,

growing old in her mother's floral apron.
Nobody says grace for the sacrifice

soon to ache her belly. Nobody has seen
a miracle. Nobody is walking on wine

across the nightclub. Nobody is losing her
coat-check ticket & slipping into the warm

sleeves of a new man's jacket. Nobody
is choking down espresso the man steeped

on the stovetop. Nobody is cold, missing
her cashmere coat in the morning.

Nobody is pleading with French
street signs to point toward home.

WHAT IS LEFT TO SAY ABOUT THE BODY

Hottest breath of July & the phone is ringing.
It's a landline. I'm alive
in another decade & about to find out

that he is not. That he will be the first
not living body I have pressed my mouth
against. Who dies of asthma

anymore? The answer is a body
named Charles that went by Chad.
A saxophone with no wind in it.

At a movie date to see *Save the Last Dance*,
he reached for his inhaler after reaching
up my shirt for the first time. After,

I stood before my bedroom mirror
shirtless, searching the small mounds
for evidence of transformation.

When his mother found his body
on the floor, his hand was not holding
the inhaler but cupping the air around it.

No, that's inaccurate, the air was
cupping his skin. The air was a heavy
blanket the whole town kept trying

to peel off all night. He could only
be touched & did nothing to the world
after that. He had no verb left.

COMPOSED

I am starting to see where the crows will dig their claws in
around my eyes, where the sun has done its mean work.
In profile I look like my prettiest aunt. Like she's lightened
her chestnut hair & tried color contacts. My grandmother's
ghost bones haunt my visage, her soft features & big eyes
I've only seen in pictures. I am contouring cheekbones
over doughy dumplings, etching charcoal across my lids
to frame what's left of their bluest fire. It's easy enough
to cake concealer over life's dark circles & blemishes
with the right tools & time. I never thought I'd make it
to see these beginnings of lines—

PORTRAIT OF MY MOTHER, AGE 56

Mom searches food labels for cancer as she passes
the age her mother's brain grew crooked branches.
In a gray minivan in a Target parking lot, she tells me
she never made a plan for retirement, never thought
she'd last that long.   & I don't shout
Look at me   I am living   I am doing this for you,
don't lower the window to Michigan's frigid progress
to ask the stars how far out the story reaches with
the two of us idling alive.   I nod, knowing
I wear the big eyes of her ghostmother. Mom waits
for me to leave her.   Three years ago I tried
to swallow a bottle of small moons & didn't call her
to say the hospital's new names   for what the hell
is wrong with me. When I finally told her on the phone
weeks later she asked if it was an accident   & I said
no   so she never asked again.   So we are silent
now   beneath the yellow glow of parking lights:
we are accomplices   or we are strangers   praying
to gods who live on dying stars   fading, flickering.

SPELL FOR UNDOING A LIFE SENTENCE

My mother is not sitting in a high school classroom
while another girl presents the week's current events.

The current events are not a dead body. My uncle's friend
doesn't tell the gas station clerk to give him the money.

Nobody is threatening to shoot. It's not a small town.
Nobody is on drugs. The cashier is not afraid.

Nobody has a gun. My uncle is not half a kite
on Mars rushing the red atmosphere,

half pumping gas into the getaway car. My uncle
did not buy the gun. Nobody is the shooter.

The cashier's shirt is not red with blood.
The cashier is not a ruined planet.

My uncle's planet is not siphoning into
a county cell. My mother is not listening

to a girl call her brother a monster. My mother
is not seeing her face locked away. My uncle does not

have her same nose, eyes, mouth. My mother isn't seeing
her monster. My uncle is not a runaway. Is never

afraid of his father's bloody belt. Is never shaking
for a fix. My uncle's fix isn't shaped like

a dead boy. My mother doesn't run
from the classroom. My uncle is not a room

she gropes about each day like she's just woken
to find the furniture's shifted without warning:

her screwup brother not next to the pool at her father's
house with the most evenly cut lawn in America,

not a whiff of pot smoke & God knows what else
burning in the garage, not a monster wearing her face

chasing her around the house with a kitchen knife
anymore. Not a joker handing her a joint

laced with rat poison to show her his bad
skies & splendors. Nobody is relieved he's gone.

ESSAY ON GUNS

I don't remember the boy's name
but I remember him swinging
through barn rafters with his brother
& me & my big brother, who was afraid
of heights but watched from the sidelines
as we all didn't fall. The boy's dad,
my dad's best friend years before
he was my dad, showed me their pig,
said they were fattening him up
to make bacon. I felt no mercy pang,
only disgust at eating such filthy animals.
This is not a story about vegetarianism.
This is about the boys I didn't see
or think of again until the bullet
misfired. The rifle they'd found
in their neighbor's garage,
up to the mischief of teenage boys
in farm country. With so much
wide open land, what prize is there
in spotting a rabbit, in disrobing corn?
I know that feeling but not the one
of holding my brother's body
with a hole in it. Not the feeling
of taking off my shirt to sop up blood
& feral howl for help *Oh God*
Oh God Oh fuck. I don't know
if the brother who lived, who first
held the gun not knowing it held death
in its chambers, grabbed his brother
plus the intent of the gun in his arms.
Or if he jumped back, heart ticking rapid
as a hummingbird, tried to breathe
with his head bobbing between knees.

Or if he bolted to the house phone,
feet pounding prayers into the earth.
I don't know if he was a cussing boy.
If he cursed God or cursed himself.
If he still does. I know his dad
drank the car away. When he called
Dad would shake his head in the sadness
of men who've been raised not to say
I ache I ache I tender I can't see
the sky through his death. The grief
of a father is a little like a bullet wound—
so much pain gushing out the body
it stains the whole world red.
Can you blame a man for wanting
a little anesthesia? For not wanting
to sit still in the carnage: his hands
that once thrust two small boys up
toward the sun. That once had two sons.

VERITY

Saint Agatha holds her breasts
               two jiggly vanilla pudding cups
         red-berry nipples plopped
             upon a silver platter. What I can't see

is the blood, the knife marks. This gory waitressing
             her task for not consenting
        to open for Quintianus. *Oh purr yes*
             he begged, but she was a shut clam.

This is supposed to be a better ending:
             to be a carved Christmas turkey
        but pure in the eyes of God. Once, I believed
           I could save a woman, called

campus police when I heard screaming
             in the apartment next door, listened
        to a lamp crash, a desk thrust over, thuds
           of a body becoming pocked

with night sky's worst ink. The door unlocked
             to a stranger in her underwear
        her lip split, meat showing. Her assailant:
           a college athlete in need

of a haircut & a better god. She asked me to stay
             near her while she pulled her bedclothes
        over her bones. The cop turned his back
           dutifully. I held her as he asked

scripted questions: *did she know the man / did he*
                       penetrate / did she say no / had she
           been drinking / had he been drinking. Agatha,
               this woman was so small, barely five foot.

Small arms, small legs, small breasts. I thought
               she was brave to banshee
       scream to wake the neighbors, but it didn't stop
               his rabid, mangy want. Agatha, I want

a painting of you with your breasts
                  as mangled cutlets on a cutting board
       a man with a white apron drowned in red.
               I want someone to tell the truth.

CLYTEMNESTRA, DAUGHTER OF LEDA, BEHOLDS A SWAN

The swan, ass up,
plunges his sharp orange
pecker into the pond
& comes up wormless—
once, twice & then
quivering pink prey
surrenders to his
serrated mouth.
Such primeval wings—
twenty-five thousand
feathers startle the air
as he flaps & struts
amid the shore muck.
I want to say his slender
neck is unremarkable—
elegance, an artist's myth.
I want him covered
in mud, hunger-thin
& molting. But here he is
swimming in beauty beneath
a blue sky, in a blue
pond, blue on dazzling
blue backdrop to his
ancient alabaster form.

DREAM WITHOUT MEN

I take a New Englander to Lake Michigan & wait
        for her to exclaim it looks like an ocean but smells wrong.
I press my nose into her blue hair, breathe in its history

of salt, make a meal of it. Pull the clothes off her body
        because it's better to let the sun learn all our pale parts.
Warm hand of wind caresses the milky slice of a ghost

spaghetti strap, the tan line a memory of days
        when modesty was king, a memory of days of kings.
In this dream there's no man in skinny jeans explaining

feminist theory to us. In this dream when our eyes lock
        it is not to say *Save me* or *I can see how exhausting it is*
to keep nodding your head for him. Boston, Minneapolis, Earth—

all the places we've drunk the sky together so far off
        I can't quite remember the feeling of her boots brushing
my calf at a basement dance party, the question of a fur coat's

past warming her shoulders as she tugs me out into the cold
        for a smoke. In this dream no men grab our hips when
the bass bumps hard. No cocks press against our asses

as we try to sing the nineties to each other. In this dream
        we are as naked & safe as we'll ever be. The way I love her
is & is not sexual. The way I love her is older than either of us.

In this dream I grab her face & say *I only want children if*
        they have your eyes. If I were to press my mouth to her thighs,
if she were to moan my name, it could not be as intimate

as it is to stand silently together digging our heels into
          heaven's coast. But it won't stay. We are sinking back into
our bodies. We drink only wine for weeks & then only milk.

We ask & ask to go back to the bright beside each other,
          but the waking world has its plans: the costs of flight,
our day jobs & night jobs & the many names for women like us.

RED SPELL

The church came predecorated with red
                petals for my mother's December wedding:
a red-hot bargain for a cocktail waitress
        who lived on bargaining. Imagine a ceremony
                of red. It must be true that a mess of red petals

runs through me like other people's children
                race through fields. Call me a red hoarder.
Red lover / red arbiter / piggish red
        rover burgling the almost-lives of
                ovum. For centuries women used the red

of poinsettias to expel a wrong red.
                (When I say expel, I mean abort.)
I've stowed this knowledge inside
        my reddest meat. A woman said it plainly
                in a poetry reading nine years ago.

I need to speak flowery. A red rage
                frightens me in Texas. There are old spells
one must hold tight. One must know
        the flowers (poinsettias / rue / pennyroyal)
                for what to do after the IUD expires,

what to do in this country of red-faced men arguing
                (again) whether Penny should rusty-knife red
dirty-dancing die on a red-soaked folding table.
        What to do when the men get to say yes (again).
                When all we have left is red.

MOUTHY

Fantasy after watching *Teeth* (2007)

Men come to me with their ugly

ploughing & I shout *Hail*

to the weedwacker, motherfucker.

Oh yes, oh I need the red, oh my poor

dizzy head, oh it spins, it spins me.

I am such a wretch without my iron

supplements. I find men's sausages

make the best lozenges.

I didn't understand it at first.

I've always been a picky eater

fed cabbage & radishes

to the family corgi

& sulked to sleep with a rumble

in my tummy. My second mouth can't help

but gnash ravenous

at the sight of a good, plump

kielbasa. Hunger shepherds

every animal. Tell me something,

Dumpling, have you deserved

all the sugar plums & arabesques

you've devoured? Have you

ever snuck into the kitchen, licked

fresh batter from an unpatrolled

spoon without asking the baker

if she'd like to share?

SELF-PORTRAIT AS MEDUSA

This is an old story I am trying on:
Let my hair be a bonnet of wriggling
serpents, venomous & poised to strike
at slightest suggestion of aggression.
Let my gaze make statues of men caught
mid-act. Some would be beautiful in form.
The baseball stud with muscled shoulders
when I was trying to nap off a spinny
drunk at sixteen while the party danced on,
the one who said *Nobody out there cares
what happens in here*—I would like his
stuck-stone body, dick hard & grinning,
placed prominently on my front lawn
hedged with unpruned, wild wild bushes.

CALLING HER NAMES

Call her crick in my neck
I thought the chiropractor fixed   Call her wolf
           that picked me up by the scruff to keep
                      as a plaything
a play, I can't figure out my lines, where the audience sits
              a plush purple chair in my past with cigarette burns
where my death sits   where she screams out
       at a man throwing me around a living room
dance party   poor swing dancer   where she screams me out
        of a cab   the man caught pouring
his martini into mine   again & again   Beauty
Bar   Chicago   Call her the love
        that eats me for breakfast   Call her the love
that asks for my hand   in tornado
        & barfly   in stomp out the room until
it's time to be a better song   Call her chaos-
lover   Call her   burns the whole damn house down
        after eviction   Call her house   Call her
changed phone number   Call her   I can't
              pull scrap metal from a field   & build
a getaway car   can't play fiddle with toxic strings   can't play
        dead anymore   Call her disaster   porn
Call her   *I'm too fucking tired to look anymore*   Call her & say
        it's okay you're okay it's okay   Call her my name

ELEGY FOR LAVINIA

Die, die, Lavinia, and thy shame with thee . . .
And, with thy shame, thy father's sorrow die!
—Shakespeare, *Titus Andronicus*

Though your words are but a scar that haunts
                          your mouth, your body collateral damage
           in the quarrels of sovereigns, hand & tongue
        hacked off by your rapists, pulse ended
by your father's noble sword, by his vision
                   of mercy—tell me, does heaven give back
      your body made whole again, the blood
        siphoned back into your arteries, your delicate
wrists intact, attached to hands, fingers offering
                to slip inside your woundless pink *yes*
        conducting tremors down to your toes, or
          do you get to be done with the body?
Of course, you had to be raped so we could get the story
                     with your assailants baked into a pie
      for their lusty queen mother to eat. This is the good part:
       she doesn't know she's eating her sons
but deserves it. What does it mean to deserve
            horror? When you walked into the woods
      alone did you consider the likelihood of horror
        coming to you? Lavinia, I wouldn't bring you back
into this world, would not pray to close your wounds
            & raise your body into a tidy target.
     The sun is the oldest searchlight. The body
       the oldest weapon. Oh, how I wish to fall
to my knees & press my cheek
           against your belly. I can't
    ask you to stay with me
     so I am begging you to leave.

FIVE DAYS BEFORE THE ELECTION

& I don't want to feel the earth today because a rich man is in it
        who says he has the right to grab

the most *mine* thing I can imagine but maybe wouldn't want to
        because maybe I am almost thirty

& have grown stately in myself these last three years,
        watched ass & breasts become

rounder worlds & said *okay, I can inhabit more*
        cells, can be the earned size

of my grandmothers. & it is American to consider
        that he has a right to lead

America, to gather the wrinkled hands of bankers
        & show them all the nooks & crannies

cloaking hushed treasures, teach them how to strip
        the quiet armor women don

when we are tired of eyes following our legs
        up staircases. I want to lie

down in a riverbed, to let the water rush over
        until I am a cold nothing,

touched only in the urgent pity of rescue
        divers dragging me

back to earth. I want to let a man, a stranger, worry
        over my body, what makes it

tick & gasp. I want to name each thigh dimple
        & raised vein, each flake

of dry skin & stubbled hair, lest someone think
        they were ownerless,

run their hand up my skirt on a bus like it wasn't
        a valued thing thieved. I want

to be precise about how rich I am, how bountiful
        my folds of skin: this museum

of a pussy, this grand opera belly. Let the government
        erect a fence around my yards

of legs, lush country of bush & blood. Let me be
        a closed border, a private club.

RUMOR HAS IT

I am a poison yes.
Do me wrong,
& I'll Pompeii you,
keep your beautiful limbs
captured in poses
you thought were private,
a little like a scientist
pinning a bug
in its place on a chart.
This is a spot for
an asshole. This
is a spot for his beautiful
shoulders. Rumor has it
I am the volcano & the orgy,
more witch than
princess, more locust plague
than breeze. Maybe it's true.
I made up stories like a god
trying to teach a lesson
on manners. I want it to be.
I want, I want, I want.

& pisses herself. Drunk Bitch drops her drink in the lap
       of a slightly less drunk body & is sure she's found love
             in his smiling shrug: *Easy, Tiger.* Drunk Bitch finds love
in the chest hair of a gyrating diplomat but loses
       her keys & coat ticket while trying to find the beat.
             Drunk Bitch's hips lie about her age & relationship status.
Drunk Bitch sees every park bench as a balance beam.
       Drunk Bitch says she used to be a gymnast & isn't lying
             but wasn't ever very good. Drunk Bitch is limber
but bruises easily. Drunk Bitch has never broken a bone
       but has broken five cellphones, three necklace clasps
             & the hearts of a squadron of decent & indecent men.
Drunk Bitch's stagger summons lust from the loins
       of unimaginative men. Drunk Bitch sips the future
             & burns the past. Drunk Bitch ladles rum punch, spills red
rumors across her blouse, & swears she's not drunk
       tonight, just clumsy. Rumor is Drunk Bitch swallowed
             the salt of a man in the bar bathroom. Drunk Bitch sloppy
paints her toenails pink until she feels pretty enough
       to text old drunk lusts. Drunk Bitch is as Drunk Bitch does.
             Drunk Bitch kisses like a vacuum mating with a wet sponge.
These days Drunk Bitch stretches her luck till it pulls.
       Drunk Bitch causes a commotion, leaves a house
             party on a stretcher. Drunk Bitch gets up to get drowned.
Drunk Bitch floods the life of the party in Drunk Bitch tears.
       Drunk Bitch clicks her heels three times & wakes in a new
             home with no clothes or cab money. Drunk Bitch watches
strangers in their underwear make coffee, eggs, sometimes
       banana waffles. Drunk Bitch still has this one good trick:
             she lies down like a corpse for four days with drawn drapes
& groans *Lazarus, Lazarus.* Drunk Bitch is the resurrection
                   & the splintered cross.

BABYLOVE

I loved how brave he was to tell the story about that woman
in the back seat   how he'd held her down decades ago
& learned never to do it again   to never force   a woman
down again   except for the others he tells me aren't real
not like that first one who was real   & taught him   never
to do it again   & it's true I was twenty-two & freaked out
after the poetry workshop   we played "never have I ever"
& I had no clothes left because I'd done everything because
I'd been bad for years   for bad years   & that was good until
I was straddling him on the couch   & didn't want to be
bad anymore   so I stood up shaking   & he said   *whatever*
you want babylove   & I wanted to put on clothes
so he gave me soccer shorts & a t-shirt   & tucked me
into the couch   & I said I wanted to sleep next to him
& he said *whatever you want babylove*   & it wasn't anything
violent   but the next time it happened   I couldn't walk
straight in the morning   but I liked it   I'm sure   I was
half-laughing when I told him   how sore I was   at brunch
I ordered a bloody mary & a pulled pork sandwich I couldn't
keep down   & felt bad he was paying   boxed up leftovers
for his roommate   & his roommate asked where I'd slept
& I said on the couch   & he said he didn't see me
on the couch   & I said *fine*   & he said he knew & it was *fine*
he wouldn't tell anyone   & this was being a gentleman
I was sure until I wasn't sure it mattered at all what I wanted
when I was pulled from the dining room drunk   & giggling
with undergrad boys   I thought were too young for me
but one of them was cute.

After the Halloween work party wearing a black slip,
>   a picture of Freud taped to the front
>   (*a Freudian Slip! hahaha! a brainy skank!*),
after proving my dominance
>   at flip cup, after the turtlenecked
>   Amelia Earhart asked if I was a stripper
(*hahaha!*), after how my body looked in lace
>   & I said I used to teach in the Ivy League
>   & drank faster—a pretty black swan drove me
home, where probably my roommate was smoking his menthols
>   on the front porch, belly gurgling with stolen wine,
>   a sous chef's easy bounty. Probably I walked sloppy
in my heels, a chicken with my head hacked off
>   bumbling senseless. Probably his long arm
>   draped around my shoulders harmless
as a dead snake. After he left my torn
>   stockings atop the washing machine—
>   I asked if he'd used a condom after I asked
if he'd fucked me & he looked down
>   at his feet, & he said no
>   he didn't like using them. I said
>   very little for a very long time.

DRUNK BITCH WANTS TO FUCK LIKE A MAN

How lush the night, draping its inky curtains
over cheekbones & pedicures. July
licking its way around every ripe calf

& thigh, wet hug of sweat
& cotton. Tube top, short shorts, cheap
bar magic. Say *Please.* Say *We are made*

of curves & glisten. Your sweetheart
is not your sweetheart. I am
the beginning & the end of this

story: Listen, it's nobody's fault. All winter
we wore the curse of the Midwest's cold
shoulder, puffy coats & chaste long

underwear. Let's show the warm patios
of Ann Arbor how it looks to take
what we want, this dream of plenty

& plenty of dream. Muddle regret
into an old-fashioned glass. Be simple
syrup sugaring the burn. Say *What if cheating*

is the most honest thing humans do. I'll ask
the softest skin of your neck what
its name is. I promise I won't remember.

covered in hives. Sometimes the body
       refuses the day's story,
screams at the news from every pore
       & hair follicle. Says *No, I will not*
consent to this invasion, I will fight
       at my own risk, break
red, smear this little trickle of blood
       across clean sheets.
& this is what I have faith in:
       the body's knowledge
of threats to its sovereignty. I can choose
       dozens of products to lessen
my response to danger. I leave the pharmacy
       with bag full of gentle
sensitive-skin lotions & ointments.
       It is good to be wrought tender
enough to feel the day's sting. Discomfort,
       a warning: *Stop this. Stop*
this before your whole body is a swollen open
       sore, a raw wreckage of neglect.

WHAT I LEFT

An old oak dresser bought on consignment
I couldn't squeeze into the moving van.
A liberal man from Alabama firing slurs
into the dizzy heart of the house,
not because he's racist or has a problem
with homosexuals—just 'cause he's got the right
to language, free speech. How he'd show me
his hunting knives & the bleached skulls
of boars. His Mad Dog. The blank threat
of everything left to violate. My security
deposit. His daily looting. My shit job
as a nostalgia peddler, editing books
that let history shine in a less grotesquely
violent light. His revised blame. My shameful
quiet. A rusted padlock. The flooded ground.

LEARNING TO LEAVE A BAD THING ALONE

I loved the story of his neck too much:
the failed noose last spring, the x-ray saying
everything's fine fine still works fine
proof against my dead friends
who choked & broke alone, the ones
I said I was done writing about.
When he mentioned his high school
nemesis, the truck set on fire,
how his dad made him work
all summer to pay back the damage,
or the face of his ex's paramour
bashed in with a board outside
his California apartment,
how the police agreed with him
—*don't poke the bear*—
it wasn't a threat, not exactly.
When he sped off, deserted me
in a city 120 miles from home
sitting at a table in Barnes & Noble
with a latte & a poetry book
certain I was texting other men—
I wagged & begged on the phone
like a dog chained in the rain all night.
When he came back, I was shaking
on a bench with perfect posture
trying to look like I wasn't
the kind of woman men abandoned.
When he pulled off the highway
down a side road, parked
on the shoulder, I thought
If this is how I die, God, so be it. But
that wasn't my ending. He held me
while I wept & cursed & wept & cursed.

I felt him get hard through thick denim
& liked it. Back in his family estate
I idled with his head in my lap all night
watching zombie movies on the couch
& knew he was my punishment.

DRUNK BITCH TRIES HER HAND AT RECOVERY

after "Drunks" by Jack McCarthy

We recover our bodies from welcome mats & the entrails of night.
We recover our keys & wallets from what we swear will be the last bar,
the last time waking up to the shaky red dawn & knowing it's inside us,
the shaking, the red, the cursed sky.
We know we are what the dawn hates
as much as we hate the dawn.
Sometimes we don't recover everything. Our coats wander off
on the backs of strangers, our debit cards swept up & trashed,
our heaven spayed, our heaven trashed.
Sometimes we're what's recovered
from the sharp rocks of gorges, from our bathroom tile, from our beds
if we're lucky. Sometimes we are lucky & recover
condom wrappers & say a little prayer to that
little bit of sense. Sometimes we are unlucky
& recover condom wrappers & say a little curse
to that common bit of theft. Sometimes
nothing gets recovered. Sometimes our life
is a maxed-out credit line, a bargain with a jackass god
we've created in our own image. Sometimes we say
fuck you & kick a wall until our toes break.
Sometimes we break the wall & the landlord levies
a fine that we've earned. Sometimes we earn
fines we don't talk about, that aren't in the books.
We bury our unrecovered, their organs ruined by the God
we've made: God of blackout drives,
of blood vomit & shits & lying to doctors,
God of falling over at work parties
& ruining nice clothes, God of ruining.
We bury our unrecovered in closed caskets
when we can. Sometimes it's best to burn them.
Sometimes the family insists
on leaving the caskets flopped open—
give the undertakers some real work.

We see how fast a face can gray.
We say *He looks god-awful.* We pray
on pavement-scarred knees
that there is a heaven for the selfish.
We try to walk it off but can't get rid of ourselves.
We sing hymns to a better God
& sob. We eat dry sheet cake in church basements
& sob. We sob in the bathroom & sneak sips
of burning quiet. Sometimes we bury ourselves.

MEDUSA WITH THE HEAD OF HARVEY WEINSTEIN

after Luciano Garbati's *Medusa with the Head of Perseus*

Garbati has carved Medusa
        buxom & lithe, the seven-foot bronze Gorgon
           of our wet dreams with muscled
                legs & buoyant tits,
hairless cunt (of course). Her stunning gaze, half moony
        wonder, half cold stone, stares out from Collect Pond Park
           across Lower Manhattan & into the courthouse
where Harvey Weinstein is tried for planting snakes
        in a young girl's jaw. Everyone with any decency loves
           how her hand grasps Perseus's thick hair, his head
        hanging down like an ornament bobbing beneath
an evergreen branch. They love her revenge
        & the crimes that have been done to her
body because she wears it all so well
        like a see-through gown. No man's holding Medusa
           by her snakes this time;
        this time her snakes are a chorus coiling
           around her face, charmed
        as we all are by her soft mouth. O Medusa,
if I were a sculptor, I would carve you holding more
        decapitated heads than your hands can bear. Where
is Poseidon slithering into you? & where
        is Athena cursing you with snakes & stones
           for daring to be raped in *her* temple?
Here is the head of Poseidon & here is the head
        of Athena & here the head of Harvey Weinstein,
        & here's a horde of heads waiting to be named.

THE ASTONISHING

thing, O Saint Christina, is how
the women keep lining up
to give testimony:

the ugly smells of sweaty beards
they cannot bear assaulting
their nostrils, what horrors

their bodies have risen
from, how they have flown
high above the earth

& burrowed fathoms deep
into its fiery core searching
for a place untouched by men.

They never find it. A man's
voice keeps asking
are you sure? Are you seeking

attention, fame, fortune
to ruin a good, God-fearing
man's life? How can we trust

your word over his? O Saint
Christina, how do I get up
there in the cathedral rafters

body pressed flat
against the boundary?
At least a bee trapped

in a closed car hurtling
its tiny mass against
the windowpane is trying

to push against a solid.
I need to desert the internet—
Kavanaugh's confirmation

scalds me. Our Christine
keeps saying, *I was pushed*
from behind into the bedroom.

I drank one beer. I was pushed
into bed. I yelled. I heard Mark
& Brett laughing loudly. His weight

was heavy. Seared into my memory
they have haunted me. O Saint
Christina, to be astonishing

might be the only rational act
for a woman. To throw
your body into a furnace,

a mill wheel, the paparazzi
& see if it's true, God
has blessed you.

A FEW MORE LINES ON LAVINIA

After they rape her they hack off her tongue & hands
        so she can't articulate
who's wronged her & how. This is an old part
        of what it means to be a woman.
I am nearly thirty & still shake sometimes walking
        alone to 7-Eleven late at night
after my roommate uses the last of the last
        roll of toilet paper. A Slurpee
in hand for good measure & a pickup truck
        honks at me crossing I-35,
as if to say *I see you & could take you but won't,*
        as if to say *look at what*
a nice guy I am. Nice guys keep me up at night,
        write rock albums about how nice
they were to me, how I had no good reason
        not to stay theirs. Lavinia,
I hate watching you suffer on stage because I know
        it doesn't end. Your shame,
the shame of having walked alone in the woods
        in a woman's body. Better
to be a wolf dressed in a grandmother's nightie,
        better to eat the men alive.

SOME THINGS WE CARRIED

after Tim O'Brien

We carried twenty-eight days of pills in small plastic dials. We carried the dates of our last periods. We carried lipsticks & pressed powder compacts. Sometimes we carried keys to buildings we didn't live in anymore. Sometimes we carried mace & feared it'd be used against us. We carried smartphones that carried the news, the weather, maps, emergency contacts. Sometimes we carried each other. Sometimes we carried a woman, the wife of a young psychology professor, after she broke down in the cocktail bar over a parade of whiskey sours. Sometimes we carried her black eye. Always we carried her rehearsed story—changing the kitchen lightbulb at a late hour, her foot slipped, head slammed against the corner of the counter—how she had to keep repeating it to friends & strangers. We carried how leaving was impossible. We carried how she was his student before she was his wife. We carried the scream of a woman in the college apartment complex, the sound of a lamp crashing against the wall, her ex-boyfriend on the rugby team who'd come back to claim her, the blood on her lips as we held her & waited for paramedics. We carried our mothers who carried us. We carried how they left until our fathers stopped drinking. We carried each other's pregnancy tests & Plan B & Monistat in CVS bags hidden beneath things we didn't really need: extra toothbrushes, deodorant, iced tea. We carried the names of children we feared having. We carried tampons & Xanax & books of poems. We carried our youths. We carried the first men to pound fists against walls next to our heads. We carried wanting to be wanted like that, like they'd break us if we weren't theirs. We carried fear each time we left. We carried our luckiness. We carried what we hadn't been charged to endure, our good teeth & bones still in place. We carried bar tabs & a series of credit cards. Sometimes we carried condoms & sometimes we carried risk. We carried each other home & said that was safer than not carrying each other home. Sometimes we carried the gentle tastes of each other's mouths. Sometimes the carrying was so gentle.

DREAD MYTH

A woman is abducted & winter is invented:
        I am six pomegranate seeds cold
this November. America lowers itself
        into a dirge that goes like this: *Grab them*
by the pussy. You can do anything. I can't
        stomach the news, research
kinder animals. Today I learned zebras
        live in harems & felt jealous
of how they surround their weak & wounded.
        A circle of stripes blends together
into a fence with no opening, protecting
        their defenseless. Not that I want to share
my partner but I want women to surround me
        when I am the weakling—this bloody nose
year, this migraine's dark orbs, this gut
        broken by medicine year. I make
my own chicken soup, stroke my own hair.
        My love never learned how to
play nurse, though one summer
        I sponge-bathed a high fever off him,
held cool rags to his neck & fed
        his fire-throat popsicles. Something tender
rules me whether or not I accept it.
        I can write Persephone immune to the lure
of Hades, say the seeds go right through her,
        stain her lips red & nothing more—
but the trees still stand naked. The sky refuses
        to abide my revisions. One friend says
to eliminate gluten & dairy, one to anoint
        myself in essential oils, one mails
mysterious bottles of herbs. Dread is opening
        a deep cave in me. I fear it
won't spit me back whole this time.

There is precisely this much hope. There is sharing
        a carnal kiss in the front seat of a new lust's car
under the dark cloak of a starless night.

& maybe, for a second, there is transcendence,
        a body rising above the windshield a little like
a ghost, swooping over a town that is less

safe than it was a week ago. There is the promised
        beauty of bellies & mouths, how infinitely
linked we can become. There is a room

filled with graduate students weeping
        for their country. For how they believed in a limit
of hate that was lower than the actual figure:

62,984,828 people who hated a woman's voice
        so much they elected a shouting caricature
of toxic masculinity. There is a professor who grabs

        my arm in the kindest way, says it's good
to not sit alone. There are still so many ways
        we can be kind to each other.

AUBADE WITH THE LONGEST EYELASHES

Running my right hand down his chest
        the first time I am astonished
by the softness of hair, the coffee

        brown & early grays of it. How lucky
the rising & falling of breath beneath ribs
        he tells me were once broken by an idea

of masculinity that never fit him. A military
        school for the poorly behaved sons of well-
to-do parents, where he was too slender,

        too epicene & kind to escape unscathed
but built a business out of cigarettes
        to cajole meatheads into protecting him

from the missiled fists of teenage rage
        homing in on a target. Praise the good
magic tucked behind healed ribs

        & a questionable tribal tattoo. Praise
the first weathered lines etched across
        his forehead, his eyelashes (so full & dark,

like a mascara commercial!) that flutter
        open when I kiss his bald head in the glow
of morning, sugar fogged & grinning. Praise

        his pretty cheekbones & pretty legs, pretty
beard—I don't know how I could ever
        get over them. The chorus of rescue dogs

is singing our wake-up song. I am begging
        them to teach me the trick to eagerness.
I used to know it. I nestle my face

into his chest, press my lips to the spot
        where his heart resides.

ON PROGENY

The powers that be are conspiring to make the ugliest
children. On television America drops the biggest

non-nuclear bomb on Afghanistan, calls it the "Mother
of All Bombs," "MOAB" for short, in case we need to speak

quickly about the distant mountain with its head
blown clean off. Putin claims to possess a bigger

device, "The Father of All Bombs" aka "FOAB"
aka "Big Daddy." I hold the small pouch of my gut

& am grateful it is not conspiring to make anything.
Medical science has made it easy to not bring new bodies

into this festering America that eats its sick & spits back
their bones. Thank you, Adam Smith & Ayn Rand

Thank you Protestant Work Ethic & Invisible
Hand. Thank you, Congressman Burgess. No, thank you,

Mr. President. I won't give you the possibilities
of the 200,000 eggs tucked snug inside the warm bed

of my belly. Not one banker or cellist. Not a single soldier.
You hear me? Deep within me, chubby legs of children

on top of children kick & race safely through rows
& rows of roses & never get pricked. Within me

river & roots, shore & stars, prayer & pasture,
symphonies I am keeping to myself.

SOME THREADS FROM A DEPRESSION

~

Lately, the world only speaks to me
            like this: the slow
failure to shove a thread through
            the eye of a needle
& each day, a new mending pile.

~

I made a promise I wanted to keep:
            to never speak to her.
To leave my dead self swallowed
            in the heavy blue
I swallowed. Four years after suicide,
            everything I touch echoes
her song: *Drown a little dream with me.*

~

Small tufts of her hair on the pillow
            each dawn so familiar
I could weep for the scent. Oh, isn't it true
            all the world's lavender
grows only for her? Maybe this is a love
            poem. Hasn't her belly
gently pressed my spine each night

~

since I left her? Some nights I try on her clothes,
            the yoga pants I woke
not wearing: the hospital replaced them
            with a backless gown
& catheter. For a year I wouldn't touch them,
            convinced the fabric smelled
of death. But I didn't throw them away,

~

Honey. I know you've been here through times
            of rape & wasting, unknotting
the world from my back. I don't know where
            this old thread leads either.
Is each soft strand more offering or omen?
            I want to say something
about the razor bites at my ankles. I want to say God,

~

get this bitch away from me. But this sob song
            suits me. Bluest. Water falling
from a showerhead, enough makeup to make
            a blue face smile, a vintage blue
dress that twirls. Oh, how I know each stitch by heart.

ODE TO CHILL PILLS

My mother used to tell me sleep would find me
in my thirties, as if sleep were a gray hair waiting

to sprout among the strands of youth.
I have no gray of my own yet. August in Texas

burned all heaven's sheep, nothing to count
toward sleep. I want to call my mother & tell her

the weather forecasts were wrong, again, the drugs
not working. That I am thirty & drenched

from brain to belly & it's her fault somehow.
I was promised these rough birds would stop

their clamor songs. Too much Donald Trump
& wildfires & insurance forms & how do I keep

the same body next to me when there are so many
lovely scents & thighs in the world. Too much,

too much. & then the dosage doubles & doubles
again, a horse pill I can barely swallow, until

a clearing yawns open between my ears so wide
my whole being could spread across it like

a bed of soft grass & it's good, so good, luxurious—
a fuzzy robe I keep donning from sleep to work

to dinner to sleep. I keep waiting to get found out.
For someone to ask, *Why are you wearing*

your bathrobe in public? Are you confused
by the meaning of business casual?

& recommend something smart,
a blouse & pencil skirt. & I'd say *Yes, I am*

very confused by meaning. But nobody minds
how slow I slink behind the soft. Some days

I barely raise my arms to wave across
the street at familiar faces, friends.

The arbiters of happiness assure me
this is better than the undrugged sob

sky. All this soft on soft, a padded room
within the mind, no sharp edges to bruise

my thoughts against. Isn't this what it means
to be lovable? Such a becoming shade of bland.

SELF-PORTRAIT AS TOO MUCH

Some nights I wait for him to fall asleep,
my arm wrapped around his chest: big spoon.
This is how we fit best together. His slender
body shudders as he travels into dreams.

As he jerks out of consciousness, I steal back my arm,
quietly slink my body to the edge of the king bed
& tiptoe to a good sobbing place. In the guest bathroom
mirror I examine how big my skin has grown.

I'm afraid I'm already too much whale for him.
I step into the bathtub half-clothed, T-shirt & panties,
curl into the smallest ball I can make, my too much
thighs pressed against my too much chest

& sob noiselessly. This is how I will lose him:
drowning alone in a bathtub with no water.

MEDUSA AS SHIELD

after Medusa *by Caravaggio*

~

I love how you've painted your own face
            as Medusa's. What isn't
                        a self-portrait? Behold how her snakes
keep biting each other after
            her head's been hacked off,
            how her horror survives beyond
the body. To see your wildness painted
            into her eyes is to see
                        my own—the pupils wide as coins,
            eyes of a spooked mule, eyes like a venomous
            lust who mistook white powder
for heaven. Who mistook me for an open door.
            Her stare disrobes me. I know
                        she sees me naked
            & coiled around a night-
wound. The O of her mouth shouts
            You will never be free of me,
or whatever wail is loosed
            when a heavy blade severs
                        head from shoulders, ribbons
of blood fraying out from the neck
            like strands of my red hair.

~

When I said a venomous lust
            I meant he sunk his teeth
            into my shoulder during a hurricane
                        & that was the sweetest thing
he ever did to me. I want it to be true
            that I, too, have the power to haunt.

It must be true that when the handsome man
            liquored me open,
                        he never looked straight at me,
            never knew my eyes
watched from another room
                        counting the minutes
            until he finished.
If it is true that he transfigured me
            vile & slithering, snakes circling
brains, halo of horrors, horror
            of halos—then let me wear their hissing
                        headband out on the town.
            I could use someone to hold my drink
& someone to bite the uninvited hand
            tracing my tattoos in dim bar light.

~

            Honey, I've been playing shield
since I was a girl. Here's how it goes:
                        I am sixteen & buying a fake
engagement ring to wear to my first job
            selling blue jeans with manufactured holes
& men twice my age
            keep mistaking my crown of snakes
for bows & ribbons.
            The zirconium ring sings
            I am owned, I am owned, let me alone,
            which is the only song the men know
                        how to hear from a girl-mouth.
Or here's how it goes:
            I am thirty-five & alone in Paris
                        & slip into a slinky new
wrap dress, twirl in the hotel mirror & change
            into something more shielding
            because I can already feel a stranger's eyes
                        examining the pale whisper where

the V-neck plunges below tan lines. I am tired
        of wearing this story. I want to slither into
                shadow, to disappear into the gloaming
        & retire my quiet armor.

~

Does my venom distress you? I am trying to
        get my snakes in order:
                I polish their fangs & brush
        their tongues like a good mother.
All my pretty vipers, my whole den
        at attention, necks snapped back, ready.
My snakes wind up my calves,
                through my womb, around
my neck. They are my crown
        of roses, my thorns & petals.
My snakes are lovers
             until they aren't.
        Our safe word is *silence*. My silences
clench my jaw until it clicks & aches.
        My snakes are my snakes.

ON WANT

Capitalism is ruining my hair but insists
I keep it long. My love likes it hanging

past my knotted shoulders. So does my father
who used to grumble woundedly each time I'd cut
its wisps to dust my chin. Mom explained once

she thought it was a sex thing, liking long hair—
so I chopped it off. These days lust won't speak to me.

Buried in drugs that keep me less angry at
it's hard to say exactly what. I want so badly
to want again. My clit, music-less,

seems to be the problem. No, the problem
is the heaviness of pills or the problem is

I have never been a steady animal, skittering
my way from job to job, state to state
love to dread, & now there is his house

& herd of hounds & Costco membership
& the loud part of me that says shave

your head, wild the night, drink the bartender
keeps waning. This emptying sky keeps me
up at night. O Moonlesss, O Dallas

Light Pollution, O God—curse me, dress me,
leave me, end me. I don't care what you do

but hurry. I'm a liar. If nobody strokes my hair
I werewolf. I devour the hours & forget all
but the scraps of cloth still stuck in my teeth.

ALL THE HEAVENS WERE A BELL

Last summer pain took a fifth of my body
            weight, seared a no into my stomach
                        with its endless please ibuprofen / please
sumatriptan / I would do anything / please
            to not revolve around this igneous planet's
                        swelling gravity closing my books, pulling
me into bed, shutting off my lights.
            Tornadoes reopened pain's red mouth
                        in my brain this week—it's natural,
my neurologist says, for weather to do this
            to me. In olden days, naturally I would have died
                        young. Always a sickly child
I wouldn't have lived to bear this lonely
            eruption. *At least you'll have a good excuse*
                        for Botox a friend says, & I am supposed
to laugh on cue because I am a woman
            with smooth skin covering the blurring
                        throb of this fitful god who rules my days
& says today will be my day of rest—
            so I take my Sabbath
                        as it is given to me: like lava
has captured me in a quiet daily
            ritual. I stay frozen at the kitchen table
                        head in hands, coffee cup half full.

ANOTHER POEM ABOUT PAIN

Doctors, YouTube yoga instructors, etc.,
tell me not to do things that hurt, so

I beg a man to scatter two bags of ice across
my bed, so I can wiggle my arms & legs

& make a numb angel. I want to feel
sexy, again, google *sex positions*

for hip injuries. They say not to
do things that hurt, so I settle

on a blow job & feel useful.
This is the new trying:

lay my body down on a bed
for seven days & seven nights

& expect no miracles, only
the steady throb of continuing.

DEAR EXTRATERRESTRIALS,

How much lavender can your dusk hold?
Do you even have dusk? Or lavender?
What about holding? I used to
when I lived far from here. My family

lives with a different sky. Do you
have family? I don't know
how to go on when the sky is like this:
endless Texas bright. Nothing

wants to live here. The grass burned
dead. No rain until the firmament
cracks open. No rain until floods
& lightning: a dark green fear spreading

across the horizon. What kind of clouds
do you have? Do any of them mean
hold close the ones you love in a walk-in closet?
Sometimes it can be good to be afraid

of the weather because it means huddling
together. Sometimes closeness is a kind
of prayer. Do you have prayer?
Do you need to ask favors of the invisible?

I think I'd like to behold you & know
if you are kind. My kind is sometimes cruel.
Once, I kicked my small brother in the chest
so hard he flew across the living room

& landed on his back, the wind stolen
from his lungs—because he wouldn't stop
tickling me, because he thought tickling
was a game. But I knew too much about losing

sovereignty over my body. Would you still
like to meet me? How does your kind decide
who gets to eat & who gets to be eaten?
Sometimes my past eats my hunger

at dinner. I sit across a table from
a beautiful man who has worshipped
every freckle on my skin & I hear my father
say I shouldn't eat anything but salad,

hold the dressing. How often do you speak to
your past? I'd like to imagine a relationship
where I close my eyes & there is no voice
repeating: *Someone ought to just put you out*

of your misery. If you have a place where
memory is a quiet blanket, will you
please swoop down from the clouds
& swaddle me new in your world?

But not too long. My love once drove me
to the top of a mountain so I would trust
him while feeling terrified. Or he drove me
so I could see how far the earth stretches.

Maybe he thought I'd like to look down
the great green slope licking the ground.
Does your kind have love? It scared me
how the roads swirled up the mountain,

how there was no rail & I could see
this life, telling him which shirt goes
with his jacket & kissing his forehead,
ending without my consent. I'm sorry.

I can't explain why we keep doing it:
pull a body into a body & say this
is the best we can do as humans.
But it's true. It's true every time.

ODE TO JOY

(Or to an Avocado Smash Artisanal Toast)

I can say with a certain degree of confidence
the remains of a beautiful avocado are decomposing
somewhere in America while elsewhere bellies cry out
for the good fat of avocados. I once held my brother
when he was still new, slack necked & soft skulled
& thought it was beautiful how much he needed me
to be kind. Today I stepped over the exploded insides
of a lizard I cannot identify in terms of taxonomy
but can identify as having died in a way that suggests
a glint of cruelty propelling the earth along its orbital path.
For many years it was believed that vaginal wetness
in females of the human species was alarming,
symptomatic of womb congestion that caused hysteria.
It was believed that women weren't made to receive
pleasure, that to need pleasure was insane, but
it's 2017 & I can order a latte & a slice of garlic toast
adorned with the smashed flesh of an avocado
for $8.00 from a Bank of America checking account
with my name on it. Maybe never a room of my own,
but a small table near the back of a coffee shop
& set of headphones. Maybe a handsome barista
makes eye contact long enough to remind me
I have a body but not long enough to worry me
about the weaknesses of its borders. Maybe I'll have
garlic breath all day but at least I have tasted
the earth's best stinking. At least I know the name
of this pungent ghost I'll carry with me from meetings
to a half-empty bus to a mattress made of memory
foam. At least I have made this one messy choice today:
                                        O Green Goop,
once I asked an ancient philosophy professor
how much choice humans have & he looked grave,
shook his head: *Very little, there is very little choice left.*

America tells me I need a mani-pedi, but I don't want
a stranger to touch my high arches. It would be too much
pleasure to have in public, too many nerve endings
shaking my whole body with a painful laughter. I am afraid
that whatever is rotting on the sidewalks in America
is going to stay there, unwashed & rancid.
I'll have to learn to love its ruined guts or not go outside
myself. At the edge of cruelty, what is it that keeps us
supporting weak necks, devising new concoctions
to make bread more desirable, spreading manure
over the gangly toes of corn? Let that be what rules me.

ENTREATY

Once I was a thicket. I'm sure
of dense thorns, the upward
please of cells toward noon sun.
                    What were you?
I need you to speak to me
abstractly. What animal lived
behind your knees? In your ribs?
                    I have held many
mice inside my brambles.
I have not minded their shit
& babies. Now I want
                    only sweet
clover. Do you have any
tucked behind your ears?
This is my *please* dance.
                    Do you like
what the wind does to me?
I do. My hair is a bird's home.
                    Touch it.

EPITHALAMION

Some nights I dream our wedding:
　　　　nobody can ever find the woman in charge
of catering, a shortage of vegetarian entrées

　　　　but no shortage of joy. The cake is all wrong,
gaudy metallic roses, none of the promised
　　　　chocolate beneath the icing's bling.

My dress is worse off: too poofy
　　　　& bedazzled. But in this dream love
is patient, love is kind. No starving bear

　　　　of a job market, no freezes on partner hires.
In dreams we're the kind of people
　　　　who can agree to futures with joint

bank accounts & matching aprons
　　　　or underpants, matching permanent
addresses. In this dream the failed death

　　　　six years ago knocks on the door
& says *Sorry, lady, wrong house.*
　　　　Sorry, I was looking for someone else.

In this dream nobody I love, not you
　　　　& not M, finds a body without
its tenant. In this dream no drown song

　　　　hovering, no dogs barking at my body's
wrong smell. In this dream I can promise
　　　　to keep a still house, can 100% guarantee

there's no damsel-monster coming for dinner.
       In this dream there are new endings,
endings I haven't already tried on

      & worn around the hospital wishing
for someone to bring me clean clothes.
       Love, here is my hand, my gallons of blood

that chose to keep rushing me into
      today. I almost missed this: your breath
steaming my neck. I'll take it. *I do, I do.*

TAPPING THERAPY

I google the word *muumuu* & am very sorry
           my life has come to this
desire for shapelessness. I am a blob
             of pain in the recliner this summer
my hip on fire, pleading for a river
             of opiates. & it gets worse:
it would not be wrong to call today's sack dress
          a *muumuu*. The doctor says
to ice my ass six times a day until
             the bursitis calms. Carol, my sweet
psychologist friend, skypes from Oregon
             to talk about pain, about bad stories
I've stored in my hip too long. She tells me
            to tap my face & chest & say
I can love myself with the pain, with the stories.
            & I sob for my uncle's bad hip, his never
enough opiates and alcohol, embalmed middle-aged
        corpse, my own young wildness—the overdose
        paramedics
            who dropped my body
                 like heavy groceries
down a steep stairwell
           & gave me a new crooked
              gait. She says I have wound shame
               into a small ball
       & stored it in my hip for years.
                   & she is right.
& my sobbing is right, but I don't know
        if the muumuu is right. If it's a form
              of acceptance
or quitting. My love comes home early from a party
        & asks what I am doing
            why I am crying

& touching my face. I say I'm busy
                    doing a weird thing
            with Carol. He wouldn't understand her
methods, would want something more scientific
            than this beautiful woman
                                instructing me
to tap my face
                    & let the old stories close.

NOTES

Page 3   "Parthenogenesis" refers to "Anna," the green anaconda in an all-female exhibit at the New England Aquarium in Boston who gave birth to two baby anacondas in 2019 despite having no contact with male snakes.

Page 8   "Easy as Pie" uses a disguised pantoum form in which the quatrains are condensed into couplets; this form was borrowed from the poem "Last Call" by Beth Bachmann.

Page 20   "Verity" references common depictions of Saint Agatha, which typically involve her holding her breasts on a serving platter. I am specifically referencing her depiction in a 1630s painting by Francisco de Zurbarán.

Page 25   "Red Spell" has an allusion to the film *Dirty Dancing*, in which the character Penny nearly dies from a back-alley abortion.

Page 26   "Mouthy" was written after watching the film *Teeth*, a darkly comedic horror film involving a woman who discovers she has vagina dentata. While being sexually assaulted, she bites off the penis of her assailant.

Page 32   "Elegy for Lavinia" is loosely based on Zbigniew Herbert's poem "Elegy for Fortinbras."

Page 33   "Five Days before the Election" is loosely inspired by "Instructions for a Body" and "The World's Guide to Beginning" by Marty McConnell.

Page 46   "Medusa with the Head of Harvey Weinstein" responds to Luciano Garbati's statue *Medusa with the Head of Perseus*, which was then poignantly installed in Collect Pond Park across from New York County Criminal Court, where Harvey Weinstein was tried.

Page 47   Italicized lines in "The Astonishing" come from Christine Blasey Ford's testimony to the US Senate Judiciary Committee alleging that then Supreme Court nominee (now Supreme Court Associate Justice) Brett Kavanaugh sexually assaulted her when they were teenagers.

Page 63   "Medusa as Shield" has an allusion to a line from Shakespeare's *Macbeth*: "all my pretty chickens." It also is written in response to Caravaggio's *Medusa*. Notably, this painting is on a literal shield and is also a self-portrait; Caravaggio used his own image for Medusa's face.

Page 66   "On Want" contains an homage to "Do not go gentle into that good night" by Dylan Thomas.

Page 67   "All the Heavens Were a Bell" borrows its title from a line in Emily Dickinson's "I felt a Funeral, in my Brain."

Page 75   "Epithalamion" borrows a line from 1 Corinthians 13:4.

ACKNOWLEDGMENTS

Permission to reproduce previously published poems is gratefully acknowledged. Some poems appeared with different titles and have gone through revisions since their original publication. The poem "Nobody Is Lost" also appeared in a chapbook, *Atomic Girl* (Tired Hearts Press, 2014).

32 Poems—"Drunk Bitch Wants to Fuck like a Man" and "What Is Left to Say about the Body"

American Poetry Journal—"Some Threads from a Depression"

American Poetry Review—"Verity"

Bennington Review—"Dread Myth"

BOAAT—"Drunk Bitch Tries Her Hand at Recovery"

Booth—"Calling Her Names"

Cherry Tree—"Elegy for Lavinia," "On Progeny," and "Ladylike: II"

Columbia Review—"Tapping Therapy"

Crab Fat—"Babylove"

Crab Orchard Review—"Easy as Pie"

Crazyhorse (now *swamp pink*)—"Essay on Guns"

DIAGRAM—"Mouthy"

DIALOGIST—"Portrait of My Mother, Age 56"

Gulf Coast (Online)—"Drunk Bitch Dreams of a Luminous Stream"

Heavy Feather Review—"After the Election I Woke Up" and "Five Days before the Election"

Indiana Review—"Nobody Is Lost"

The Journal—"Another Poem about Pain"

minnesota review—"What I Left"

Missouri Review—"Window Shopping"

The Offing—"Ladylike: I"

Pleiades—"Dream without Men"

Poetry Magazine—"Parthenogenesis"

The Puritan (now *The Ex-Puritan*)—"On Want"

Redivider—"Spell for Undoing a Life Sentence"

Sixth Finch—"Dear Extraterrestrials,"

TriQuarterly—"Some Things We Carried"

Underblong—"Harm's Way"

Up North Lit—"Epithalamion" and "Ode to Joy"

West Branch—"A Few More Lines on Lavinia"

Yemassee—"Learning to Leave a Bad Thing Alone"

THANK YOU

Thank you to Marisa Siegel, Jameka Williams, and everyone at Northwestern University Press for believing in this vision and helping me to put this book into the world.

Thank you to my dissertation committee at the University of North Texas—Jehanne Dubrow, Corey Marks, and Bruce Bond—for the guidance they provided toward revising this book. Thank you to my workshop peers at the University of North Texas for their invaluable input on poems from this collection, especially Matt Morton, Sebastián H. Páramo, Jim Redmond, Joshua Jones, Andrew Koch, Leah Tieger, Kimberly Gibson, Lauren Pilcher, M. J. Arlett, Brian Clifton, Minadora Macheret, Aza Pace, and Kat Moore.

Thank you to Phillip B. Williams, Jennifer Givhan, and KMA Sullivan for their input on early drafts of this manuscript. Thank you to my workshop leaders at the Sewanee Writers' Conference, Carl Phillips, and Tarfia Faizullah, as well as my workshop peers, for their help with editing some of the final poems for this collection. Thank you to the Sundress Academy for the Arts writer-in-residence program at Firefly Farms, which provided me with the time and space needed to write and revise these poems.

And a thousand thank-yous to my wonderful husband, Jordan Frith, for supporting me emotionally through the long, several-year process of writing and revising this book, even when I wanted to give up on it. Thank you to my dogs—Daisy, Tinkerbell, and Peaches—for being my constant writing companions and for their abounding snuggles when writing these poems inevitably made me cry.